CIRCUS & CARNIVAL TRUCKS

1923 THROUGH 2000
PHOTO ARCHIVE

Bill Rhodes

Iconografix
Photo Archive Series

Iconografix
PO Box 446
Hudson, Wisconsin 54016 USA

Library of Congress Card Number: 2001131360

ISBN 1-58388-048-8

01 02 03 04 05 06 07 5 4 3 2 1

Printed in China

Cover and book design by Shawn Glidden

Copy editing by Dylan Frautschi

COVER PHOTO: A 1961 GMC truck carries the "blood sweating" hippopotamus, "from the river Nile." Hippos secrete a slightly pink body oil which quickly inspired circus owners to coin the phrase "blood sweating" to increase curiosity about the beast. The biblical name Goliath was often used for large animals, implying an intimidating creature. The beast might actually be a fairly tame female. The truck arrives on the lot with three of the side panels raised providing ventilation for the animal. Hippos spend a large part of their time in water so the rear of the trailer contains a water tub large enough for it to immerse. The rack on top of the trailer is for storage of hay which the circus purchased in quantity. The hippo was presented as a midway attraction for a small extra admission, apart from the regular circus performance. GM offered several versions of their then new big V6 gasoline engine in these trucks, matched with a five-speed transmission.

BOOK PROPOSALS

Iconografix is a publishing company specializing in books for transportation enthusiasts. We publish in a number of different areas, including Automobiles, Auto Racing, Buses, Construction Equipment, Emergency Equipment, Farming Equipment, Railroads & Trucks. The Iconografix imprint is constantly growing and expanding into new subject areas.

Authors, editors, and knowledgeable enthusiasts in the field of transportation history are invited to contact the Editorial Department at Iconografix, Inc., PO Box 446, Hudson, WI 54016.

DEDICATION

To my parents, who tolerated a kid that went to the circus when he should have been in school.

ACKNOWLEDGMENTS

Several people of the circus and carnival have contributed valuable data and oral histories used in the preparation of this book. They are: David Blanchfield, Wesley Brown, Don Kidder, Ed Lester, Bob MacDougall, Ollie Miller, Henry and Sally Payne, Gus Taliaferro, James Dawson a.k.a. "Peg" Tyrell, and Tommy White. Their friendship and assistance is acknowledged with gratitude.

My fellow members of the American Truck Historical Society have generously assisted in identifying many of the older trucks appearing in the photographs. Their expertise is greatly appreciated.

INTRODUCTION

The circus and carnival have historically been travelling organizations appearing briefly in a city or town and moving on when the potential for paying patrons was exhausted. For the circus, a single day was and is the rule. They moved every night. Logistics of transportation have therefore been an important part of these organizations. The result was development of specialized vehicles to meet the unique needs of each show, first wagons, then railroad equipment and finally trucks and tractors.

The tent circus preceded the carnival midway by nearly a hundred years; consequently, their earliest modes of transportation were more primitive. Wild animal cages and the ornate wagons for parades were dragged by horse teams over muddy country roads along with the wagons loaded with tents, seats and other baggage. Conditions of transportation limited the distances that could be traveled in a night and consequently limited the size of the show. From the beginning, circus owners were looking for better ways to transport their shows. Larger cities were farther apart. If the circus could travel faster, then it could skip the small villages and attract larger audiences.

As railroads appeared, they seemed to provide a solution, but prior to the Civil War they were not standardized. Cars, couplings and track widths were different for each railroad company. Cars owned by a railroad had to stay on that railroad. Attempts to transport a circus by rail overnight became nightmares of repeated loading and unloading cars from one railroad system to another. None were successful. Steamboats were tried and worked well for a few shows, but the audience market was limited to river towns. Most circuses moved by horse and wagon.

Of necessity, wars produce technical advances. One result of the Civil War was standardization of railroads. The Union built temporary military railroads to supply the armies as soon as territory was secured. As with everything in the military, these were built to army standards. The northern railroads were also at capacity moving war supplies and realized the value of being able to exchange cars among systems without unloading them. They also adopted standards. When the Civil War ended, America was ready for the circus train. P. T. Barnum's circus was the first to successfully adapt to rail movements. Other circus owners quickly followed and the railroad became the standard means of transportation for circuses of all sizes. The circus traveled between cities by rail; horse teams moved it from the rail yard to the show grounds. Arrival of a circus train became a major community event. One writer observed the crowd watching a circus train being unloaded and speculated that if they had fenced the track, as many tickets could be sold there as at the performance.

As with the Civil War, WWI also produced rapid technical advances. One of interest to the show owner was improvement of the motor truck. Like the circus, the army had to move on a fast schedule. The best commercial trucks were adapted to military service and the first trucks specially designed for the army went into production. Trucks that were larger, more powerful, and especially, more reliable became available. These did not go unnoticed by the circus owners

who were feeding horses, in some cases hundreds of horses, all winter when they did little work. Trucks could be stored until spring, incurring no operating expense. Trucks could pull more than they could carry. Wagons were the universal means of drayage so there were lots of them. Trucks were regularly used to pull one or more. This could be done on the circus as well. By the end of WWI several of the large railroad circuses were trying trucks to move their wagons in the street. For a time the trucks were on trial. Horses did most of the work and were the only means of loading the flat cars and spotting wagons on a dirt lot. Horse teams were also essential for parades. For the circus they were a source of pride. Handsome teams were much admired by the public. Just as most men today think of themselves as being at least marginal car experts, in the heyday of the circus they were self-appointed horse experts. In displaying fine horses, even draft horses, the circus was appealing to the same sort of interest that attracts fans to car races today. It would be many years before the circus would abandon its draft horses entirely.

For rail transported circuses, heavy trucks served primarily as tractors, towing long strings of wagons through the streets between the show grounds and the rail siding. The usual load was a flat car of wagons, unless there were hills or sharp turns on the route. An extra truck would be stationed at steep hills to help by pushing the wagon trains up. Down hill, it would be chained to the last wagon for added braking. With such heavy loads, substantial weight (termed "adhesive weight"), was needed on the drive wheels to prevent slipping. Tanks of water served this purpose very well and most of the rail show trucks were thus equipped. The water trucks had pumps, hoses and spray nozzles to supply water where needed at the circus and to settle dust. Larger shows with many trucks had other types of bodies but most were water tanks.

Shows that moved over the highway had trucks that carried all the loads formerly carried in wagons. Some were highly specialized, with bodies designed and often built by the circus. The water trucks now carried cranes to load rolls of canvas or machines to drive and pull up stakes. The weight of the tank of water served to stabilize the truck from tilting. Some trucks loaded and unloaded the tent canvas from large reels mounted in the truck body. Food service for both employees and patrons was transferred from tents to trucks, reducing the labor to set them up. Some performers used highly modified trucks as props for their acts. In the early 1950s the Al G. Kelly and Miller Bros. Circus used their trucks as rolling billboards. Most circuses had the name in large letters on each truck but this show had a different act or animal displayed there. When the caravan reached town in the morning it was routed down the main street or around the town square before it went to the show grounds. Thus, everyone saw a preview of the show. Circus trucks were and are as varied and colorful as any on the road.

The carnival, a varied collection of attractions, including rides, shows and games, did not appear until the twentieth century was at hand. It apparently originated when several exhibitors at the Chicago World's Fair of 1892-1893 decided to continue in business after the fair closed. They moved their attractions as a group to other cities where they would operate for an extended period, probably until business declined. They prospered and inevitably, competition appeared and an industry was born. Evidently most, if not all, of the early carnivals traveled by railroad. The system of loading had already been perfected by the circus companies; they needed only to copy it. But carnivals did not plan to move on a daily basis, as did the circus. The midway would be open for a week or more in each location. They would operate through Saturday and move on Sunday. To most owners this did not warrant owning a stable of horse teams, which would eat all week and work only on weekends. Instead they hired dray teams in each town. When trucks, and later tractors, became widely available, they hired those. By hiring available local transportation the carnival people became pioneers, evaluating new equipment in every city. Eventually the cost of hiring local teamsters to work from midnight Saturday until dawn Sunday had increased to the point where carnival owners were considering owning their own motive power. By the mid-1930s industrial tractors of the four-wheel type were marketed with inflated tires suitable for use off pavement. Carnivals began to buy them to load the trains. Caterpillar tractors had been rented and were subsequently purchased for use on the show grounds, which were typically dirt. Trucks still were hired locally if needed, but many locations had rail sidings nearby and the show-owned tractors were sufficient.

Following WWII, major changes affected the outdoor amusement industry. Improvements in the national highway system, started by the Works Projects Administration in the depression years, were rapidly advanced and the interstate system was underway. Truck manufacturers offered larger, heavier trucks, many powered by a new generation of diesel engines which provided reduced fuel consumption and increased life compared to the standard gasoline engines. The expanding truck industry caused a gradual decline in railroad service. They became bulk haulers. Stations in small towns were closed and freight sidings were removed. Branch lines were abandoned. Towns all over America could no longer accommodate a railroad show.

Circus and carnival owners faced the inevitable. Most of the rail shows converted to trucks; a few did not survive. Today, only two units of Ringling Bros. Barnum and Bailey Circus and one carnival, the James E. Strates Shows, travel by rail. These are very large shows for which rail travel is practical. They play larger cities where full rail service is available. Many carnivals do not have a full season of fairs and celebrations, which are their main source of revenue, and appear in shopping mall parking lots to fill in their summer schedule. For such dates, revenues are better if they split the show and play more than one location at a time. This is more practical with a truck show than with a show loaded on a single train.

Today, further changes are seen. The new generation of exotic circuses is enjoying success. They play the larger cities and remain a week or more. Carnivals have done this since inception. With such infrequent moves, owning a fleet of trucks to transport the show is not always justified. Just as carnivals hired horses and trucks in the past, carnivals and the new generation circuses are beginning to utilize commercial truckers to move their trailers. They avoid the investment, the maintenance, the insurance and the need to license employees as truck drivers. How far this trend will go remains to be seen.

Notes on the photo captions: Captions for the photos contain technical data on the trucks illustrated wherever this is available. However, many popular trucks are now "assembled" products. These are assembled from stock components supplied by specialists in the manufacture of the item. The company whose name appears on the truck may have only built the frame, cab, and hood. The number of engine, transmission, axle and other options available is extensive. However, accurate technical data could only be included if access to sales records of the truck itself were possible. Such was not generally the case and no data is given.

Captions include terms unique to the subject of circus and carnival trucks. These are defined below for convenience of the reader.

ADHESIVE WEIGHT. The weight on the drive wheels of a vehicle which limits traction or pulling force. The maximum pulling force is determined by the weight multiplied by a number representing the friction of the ground surface. The number is always less than one so a tractor cannot exert a pulling force greater than the weight on its powered wheels. The number can be as high as 0.9 for a Caterpillar on dry ground and less than 0.5 for a wheel on mud or snow. Weight on non-driving wheels does not count.

BACK DOOR. The performers entrance to the big top, usually next to the bandstand, as opposed to the front door where patrons enter.

BANNER BOARDS. A wooden board attached to the side of a circus truck water tank so that sheets of paper or cloth could be temporarily attached with tacks. The sheets carried paid advertising, painted by the circus "artist" soliciting business for local merchants. These were changed every day, since the circus appeared in a new town each day. Advertising banners were also displayed in the big top. The practice has disappeared today.

BANNER LINE. A row of very large illustrations on canvas suspended from poles or located on the side of a truck or wagon. The illustrations depict acts presented in the tent behind the banner line.

BIG TOP. The principal circus tent in which the performance is presented. A tent consists of canvas top and sides, and wooden poles and stakes. The top is by far the largest part so the entire tent is usually called a top.

BILLING CREW. The advertising crew which traveled ahead of the show to announce its pending arrival. These were mostly billposters. They were also called the "advance."

BULL RINGS. Steel rings mounted on all four corners of a show wagon, allowing it to be pulled with a rope and hook. Trucks are also equipped with them on the front. These allow the vehicle to be towed along a flat car by a tractor on the ground. They also permit an extra towing tractor in mud.

CANNON ACT. A feature where the performer is launched from an imitation cannon, on a long high trajectory, to land on a net or air bag. The cannon barrel contains a mechanical catapult powered by elastic bands, springs or a compressed fluid. A powder charge is exploded at the muzzle for effect.

CENTER POLE. The tallest poles in a tent. These are typically arranged in a row on the center line of a long tent.

COOKHOUSE. A dining facility operated by the circus for employees who receive meals as part compensation. The official names are dining department or hotel.

CROSSING. The intersection of street and railroad track where the flat cars are unloaded. See RUNS.

DARK RIDE. A midway amusement where riders are carried on small carts through a winding tunnel in near darkness. Halloween-type figures appear to frighten them.

DEAD MAN. A strong anchoring point usually used to terminate the main cable that runs the length of the big top. A dead man may be a heavy truck or tractor, an array of stakes connected together, or even a large tree.

F-HEAD ENGINE. A gasoline engine having one overhead valve and one side valve for each cylinder.

GAS CUT. A group of flat cars, usually eight to ten, parked and unloaded as a unit, which carry the trucks and tractors along with wagons. The gas cut is loaded last and unloaded first.

GREASE JOINT. A lunch counter or fast food service.

HAMMER BOARD. Part of a mechanical stake driver. The board extends upward from the hammer weight and is used to lift the weight.

HAUL. The distance from the crossing to the show grounds, expressed in miles or simply as a long or short haul.

HOT BOX. 1. A small sleeping compartment in a truck or wagon, often with only a single door or window and little ventilation, hence the name. 2. An electrical junction box, usually with a breaker and multiple outlets.

HOT WAGON. A wagon or truck on the show grounds which carries electrical generating equipment. Electrical systems for the train have other names.

HUMAN PROJECTILE. The performer in a cannon act.

JUGHEAD. A gasoline engine configuration, which was popular prior to 1930. The design overcame the problem of cylinder head gasket failure by eliminating the gasket. Engines were of the L-head or flat-head design. Cylinders and heads were cast in one piece, as individual cylinders or in pairs. Valves were inserted through plugs in the top. The smooth, rounded shape resembled a jug, the plugs suggested a cork, hence the nickname. The name "jughead" is most often applied to the Mack AC engine, although other engines were built this way. In the early 1930s, as reliable gaskets became available, the AC engine was re-designed with separate cylinder heads. The latter engines had a tall, square-edged head configuration and were nicknamed the "top hat," or "high hat" engine.

L-HEAD ENGINE. (also FLAT-HEAD ENGINE). A gasoline engine having both valves for each cylinder in the block on the same side of the cylinder.

LOADING LENGTH. The number of feet of flat car length required by a particular vehicle.

LOT. The location of a circus or carnival whether it is a vacant field, fairgrounds, park or other space.

MIDWAY FRONT. A tall, well-decorated and illuminated arch over the entrance to a carnival midway.

RUNS. Pairs of long flat plank assemblies used to form a ramp from the end of a flat car to the street, allowing vehicles to be loaded or unloaded. Also used to refer to the location where unloading is being done.

SIDE POLE. One of a row of short poles which circle the edge of a tent.

SPOOL TRUCK. A truck mounting one or two large reels capable of winding in strips of the folded canvas tent top. The reels or spools are powered by the truck PTO.

STAKE JACK. An elephant powered mechanical device used to extract tent stakes.

TRANSFER CASE. A second or compound transmission receiving power from the output of the main transmission. The transfer case has shaft outputs for all the axles and means of disconnecting the steering axle for highway use. Army trucks had an arrangement where the front axle had to be engaged when the transfer case was in low range, i.e. low gear.

WAGON POLE. The long bar extending from the front axle of a wagon, used to pull and steer the wagon. Farm boys would call it a wagon tongue.

WICKIE WAGON. The wagon carrying the lighting system which illuminates the flat cars when they are loaded at night. Also called the "shanty."

WINTER QUARTERS. The permanent office and address of a circus or carnival, with facilities for storing equipment during the winter layover.

YARD SPOTTER. A special type of truck used to move and park semi trailers at factories, warehouses and rail yards. Spotters are not intended for high-speed highway service.

The following abbreviations are used in the text:

PTO. Power Take Off. A rotating shaft extending from the transmission allowing the vehicle engine to drive accessories.

HP. Horsepower. Usually peak or gross horsepower is quoted.

RPM. Revolutions per minute. The rotating speed of the engine.

WW. World War followed by a Roman numeral denoting which war.

6X6/4X4. The first numeral denotes the number of wheels on the vehicle, the second numeral indicates the number driven.

Three Mack AC4 trucks are parked outside the winter quarters shop, ready for the 1941 season. Cole Bros. Circus had been advertising for parts or rebuilt engines and had done a complete overhaul. It was a fortunate decision. The nation would be at war by the end of the year and these trucks would have to move the circus until new trucks would be available when the war ended. The trucks were painted different colors that year. These were orange, blue, and red with whitewall tires. The latter seemed to be a useless bit of trim. The tires wore out on the sidewalls before the tread wore out. This was caused by rubbing the frame of the flat cars when they were loaded on the train. The plywood panels attached to the sides of the water tank of truck number 2 are called "banner boards." Banner salesmen approached local businesses soliciting advertising to be tacked to the sides of the trucks, thus earning more money for the show. Trucks moved around and were seen by more local people than wagons. Petroleum companies were frequent advertisers and their ads usually included an endorsement of their product by the circus.

This well equipped Mack AC was the fourth heavy truck on the Cole Bros. Circus. It had a water tank with the pump mounted on the running board. It also had a Tulsa Winch and crane, so it could be used as a wrecker or stake puller. The Metropolitan Winter Cab had the windows and doors removed since the tent circus is a warm-weather business. Note the sidewall damage on the rear tire from contact with the railroad flat car.

Mack AC number 136 was the longest and oldest in the Ringling's fleet of bulldogs. This 1923 model photographed in 1942 was painted green, as were all the trucks and cookhouse wagons. This was part of a reported agreement where the circus would make the cookhouse and trucks, most of which could carry water, available to the government in case of an air raid. In return, the circus received a fuel and tire ration during WWII. Truck 136 carried the alternate set of big top stakes and, after the train was unloaded, went downtown for ice for the air-conditioned big top.

A Caterpillar tractor adds a third wagon to the load as this Mack AC prepares to tow the string of wagons to the crossing. These wagons contain electrical equipment and reserve seat chairs, which have been removed from the big top in the background. Cole Bros.' Mack AC4s were late 1920s models and had the original AC engines with integral cylinders and heads. The rounded contour earned them the name "Jugheads."

This neat looking Mack AC number 231 is a former Al G. Barnes Circus truck shown working for Ringling Bros. It has a new diesel engine and a new steel water tank. It is parked by the circus cookhouse and has been designated as "cookhouse water," although its main duty is towing wagons.

Trucks were loaded on the "gas cut" of flat cars with the last string of wagons brought from the lot. In the morning they could tow the same wagons off the train and go on to the lot. This Cummins Diesel-powered, mid-1940s Mack LJ has the stake and chain wagon number 90 and two wagons with the big top canvas. On the side of wagon number 90 are two stake jacks used for pulling stakes out of the ground.

When new trucks were available after WWII the Dailey Bros. Circus added two of these Mack EH models. These had the six-cylinder Mack EN 354 gasoline engine and a five-speed transmission. It appears that this one, a 1948 model, had extra bumpers added so it may safely push as well as pull loads.

Mack FT number 237 comes off the train with one wagon. Other wagons will be added before it goes to the lot. The F series was the last group of chain-drive trucks produced by Mack. They were marketed for heavy construction, logging and mining work. This 1948 model has an oversize radiator, high clearance fenders and double bumpers. The original wheels appear to have been replaced by smaller ones to meet clearances between the sides of the flat car. The FT had a six-cylinder Mack EN 510 gasoline engine and a five-speed transmission.

Mack AC4 number 230 couples to a string of wagons for a trip to the lot. Truck number 230, a late 1920s model, had a water tank and a Cummins HB 400 diesel engine installed by the circus. The engine was rated at 100 horsepower at 1800 rpm and provided air brakes and electric starting.

This 1952 Mack LJ number 233 raises a cloud of dust as it leaves the lot with a LaCrosse flat wagon carrying Caterpillar tractor A5. This combination will go on the flat cars of the first section of the circus train and be the first on the lot in the next town where the circus will appear. Mack LJ number 233 had a Cummins HRB diesel engine.

Mack number 233 moves along the flat cars with the tractor on wagon D1. The first section of flats was loaded in the early evening since it carried nothing related to the performance. The Cummins HRB engine was rated at 165 hp at 1800 rpm.

The Royal American Shows carnival employed four Mack AC4 trucks to move its wagons between the show grounds and the rail yard. The first wagon behind this truck housed an early computer, which allowed the carnival management to know the attendance and revenues from each attraction soon after the midway closed each day. The truck is a 1932 model.

Mack AC4 T21 is parked on the crossing street with a long string of wagons. The first two behind the truck are large diesel generators, which illuminate the midway at night. The sides fold down to form a platform for access to the generators and switch gear. The light towers are folded on top of the wagons. This 1923 truck finished the 1958 season.

Mack diesel T21A was the "mechanics truck," carrying parts and supplies to maintain the many trucks, tractors and ride motors used by the carnival. It was the last of the old Mack AC trucks still running on any show. The late 1920s model was photographed here in 1959, still working.

A 1932 Mack diesel T18W carried a welding generator used by the carnival maintenance department, providing a mobile facility for arc welding as well as adhesive weight on the drive wheels when the truck was used to tow wagons.

This former military half-track has been converted to a double hammer stake driver by the circus. It could also be used to tow wagons both on and off the lot due to its high traction capability. It is being coupled to cookhouse wagon 6, which is part of its load on the train.

Mack number 237 moves across the lot with cookhouse wagon number 7 and stake driver number 108. The water tank on truck number 237 has been tilted slightly forward to be fully drained by the pump, which draws water at the front corner. This gives the truck a sway back look. The stake driver number 108 has two mechanical hammers driven by a Hercules gas engine and was pulled around the lot by a tractor or a team of elephants.

Mack LJ number 1 tows wagon numbers 40 and 42 carrying the wild animal menagerie tent. At the rear, between the extended poles, is a two-wheel single hammer stake driver. This 1947 LJ had a Mack EN 510 six-cylinder gas engine and a ten-speed transmission.

This 1932 Mack diesel T18W climbs the runs pulling a string of wagons. The taut cable extending across the foreground indicates that the truck is getting some help from a tractor on the ground to the right, out of the photo. T18W indicates a truck, 18 feet loading length, with a water tank.

A D4 Caterpillar tractor is ready to help Mack T21 with its load. Trucks pulled the maximum number of wagons on the train in order to steer the front wagon. Wagons loaded without a vehicle to steer had to be steered by hand.

The Clyde Beatty Circus used this late 1940s International KB 10 with a water tank and a bin on top of it for storage of all sorts of accessories. Loaded in front of the KB 10 is the train light plant, or "wickie wagon." Truck 20 appears to be a late 1940s International K6.

This army surplus Studebaker 6X6 model US6 was used by this carnival to tow wagons and carry fences and some of the midway front. It had a Hercules six-cylinder JXD gas engine producing 87 hp at 2400 rpm. A five-speed transmission with the usual two-range transfer case was standard. This Studebaker military truck is rare since much of the WWII production was exported to the Russian army.

This White M2A1 army half-track has been converted to mount a two-hammer stake driver by the circus. It is shown circling the big top area, driving pairs of stakes. The two hammer-boards are in the raised position so stakes can be inserted in the guides. Evidently, two local kids are earning tickets by throwing stakes from the bin above the driver. The White half-track had a six-cylinder White 160AX gas engine producing 147 hp at 3000 rpm. The transmission offered four speeds with a two-range transfer case. Speeds in high range were 9, 17, 26 and 45 mph. Low range provided 3, 6, 10 and 18 mph. The tracks were rubber, molded over a steel cord, so they could be operated on pavement without damage.

This 1926 Mack AC is equipped with a water tank, pump and hose reel, no doubt to satisfy local fire marshals who liked to see some sort of fire-fighting capability on the midway. These trucks would not set records going to a fire. Top speeds in the four gears with the 1800 rpm Cummins engine were 3, 6, 11 and 20 mph.

Cole Bros. fleet of Mack trucks waits on a side street for cage wagons from the animal menagerie. The animals were removed and the tent struck as soon as the last performance began. The LJ model on the right was new in 1947. The AC models were from the late 1920s.

This Mack LJ has hauled the circus steam calliope to a downtown park. Music will be played during the lunch hour as a promotional event. The truck tank provides water for the steam boiler. It is not easy to ignore the sound of a steam calliope echoing among the tall buildings. There was a ticket booth nearby to serve those inspired by the circus music.

Cole Bros. Circus 1949 Chevrolet truck number 2 prepares to tow three of the midway vendors' wagons off the lot. This truck had a Chevrolet "Load Master" six-cylinder gas engine producing 102 hp at 3600 rpm. The transmission had four speeds with a two-speed axle. The wagons had sides that raised, providing serving counters. Food, drinks and souvenirs were sold. Electric signs advertising the wares are folded on the roofs.

Mack AC truck number 4 has remained on the lot to move the stake driver. Normally it would return to the crossing to pick up another string of wagons, but the tractor that usually pulls the stake driver has not arrived and the stake row is needed as soon as possible. Note the water hose passing over the cab to the radiator, which must be leaking. The Caterpillar on the left is spotting the center pole wagon.

Dailey Bros. Circus circa 1940 Chevrolet number 16 is loaded behind the pole wagon. It is secured by wheel chocks and chains as well. This was standard practice for vehicles on the ends of rail cars to prevent the wheels from rolling over the end and wedging between the cars.

Patrons leave the circus grounds as the last performance ends. Two Mack trucks wait for wagons to come from the big top as the seats and props are dismantled. Drivers have left the motors running rather than hand crank them again. The big (472 cu. in.) four-cylinder AC engine was tough to pull over by hand even though the compression ratio was only 3.5:1.

This Mack AC mechanics truck is parked by an old water wagon used primarily to sprinkle the grounds and settle dust. It still has the driver's seat and footboard from horse-drawn days. The truck driver is drying his trousers on the front bumper. Carnivals move only once a week and sometimes less often, so the trucks and wagons last a long time.

A GMC tank truck eases down the runs with the big top pole wagon. The truck carries lots of spare tires and what appears to be the entire big top canvas crew. The large guard over the front bumper indicates that the truck was prepared to push wagons as well as pull them.

Truck number 234, a Mack LJ, makes a left turn to the lot with two of the folding seat wagons. Folded chairs cover the outside of each wagon. Truck 234 was a 1951 model with a Cummins HRB diesel engine. The automobile in the center lane is a late 1940s Studebaker.

A neat looking 1993 Ford CF 8000 Cargo truck rolls off the flat car with several wagons in tow. It has a Ford 6.6L diesel engine. The body of this truck is a self-powered freezer. In addition to providing plenty of adhesive weight on the drive wheels, the freezer preserves perishable foods for the circus diner and animals.

This bright yellow 1987 Ford F700 waits on the flat car until the train is parked. It has the usual water tank over the rear wheels and a storage box behind the cab, the big Ford V-8 370 gas engine, five-speed transmission and two-speed axle.

Truck number 237, a 1979 Chevrolet 70 with a 160 hp V-8 350 gas engine, waits in the rail yard for its next load of wagons. Flashing orange lights are used on top of the cab to indicate a towed vehicle following the truck. This was the first of the medium-duty trucks added to the indoor circus units, replacing lighter vehicles previously used.

This little truck is a UNIMOG 411 built by Mercedes-Benz in Germany. The name UNIMOG is an acronym for the German, translated "All-purpose Motor Device." It had a four-cylinder Mercedes diesel engine providing 38 hp at 2750 rpm. The transmission had six forward and two reverse speeds. Both axles were driven and had differential locks. Gross weight was less than 8,000 lbs., but it was efficient when towing wagons. The circus has mounted a welding generator on this one so it may be used as a maintenance vehicle as well.

This circa 1950 GMC tank truck has a winch and crane mounted on the front of the frame, used to load rolls of canvas in the wagons. Behind it is the "hot wagon," the diesel-electric generating system. Following that is a smaller GMC truck with a stake bin and single hammer stake driver.

The GMC canvas boom truck arrives on the lot with three wagons. The truck is a circa-1950 model with GM's six-cylinder gas engine. The last wagon is the office/ticket wagon.

The WWII 1/4-ton 4X4 truck, better known as the Jeep, gained great popularity after the war and soon found its way to the circus. Some of Ringling Bros. fleet of 1948 Jeeps are shown. These worked primarily with the power take-off shafts mounted at the rear. The PTO was a post-war feature offered by Willys-Overland, intended to appeal to farmers. What appear to be roll bars were installed by the circus to allow the Jeeps to drive under the big top canvas while spread on the ground. Thus, the Jeeps could each reach a center pole where its PTO could plug into a winch and raise the tent.

The PTO shaft of this early 1950s Jeep CJ-5 is plugged into one of the folding seat wagons providing power to unfold it. The CJ-5 had a "Hurricane" four-cylinder F-head gas engine rated at 75 hp at 4000 rpm.

A row of seat wagons have their side panels raised as unfolding proceeds. The Jeep has just connected its PTO to another one; the shaft is visible just above the Jeep headlights. This Jeep resembles the wartime model MB (or Ford GPW) and had a Willys L-head gas engine, 54 hp at 4000 rpm.

The Ringling stake driving equipment included this Jeep CJ-6 with a single hammer driver. The CJ-6 was a long wheelbase version of the standard CJ-5 Jeep. Wagon 108 and the half-track at left have double hammer drivers.

Jeeps play many roles for the circus, in many disguises. This one portrays a "Little Red School House," a performance prop. When Jeeps and tractors accumulated many miles or hours of service and were replaced by new ones, they sometimes finished their service in a less strenuous capacity such as this.

This early 1940s Chevrolet truck number 16 had its work cut out for it trying to move wagons on a soft lot. A pair of elephants in harness give the extra pull necessary. The row of poles in the background will support the side show banner line. To preserve the colors, the illustrations on canvas will not be hoisted up until the midway is open.

The tent circus is basically a summertime business but Cole Bros. Circus found it otherwise when they returned to quarters in 1948. They unloaded in a blowing snowstorm. Slick conditions limited the truck to one wagon in tow; normally it would have taken three or four. The driver certainly wished that Metropolitan Winter cab had not had the doors and windows removed.

This early 1950s GMC pole truck gets some help as poles are unloaded on a foggy wet morning. Another work elephant enjoys a snack of tall wet grass while waiting her turn to help another truck. Many shows would hire a local farmer to mow the grass the day before the circus day. Some abandoned the practice during the 1950s as a cost-saving adjustment.

This Chevrolet tank truck gets a push from an elephant on a wet lot. Behind the cab is a winch and hoist used to pull stakes. Water trucks were often equipped with hoists or cranes for lifting since a full water tank stabilized the truck, preventing tilting when an off-center load was raised. This truck is a mid-1940s model; the Chevrolet behind it is a mid-1930s model.

An early 1950s model GMC truck waits while an elephant helps another GMC truck out of the way. In the background, the big top center poles are already up. The trainer stands off to the left indicating that the elephant responds well to voice commands.

This tandem axle early 1990s Kenworth truck carried nearly all components of a major ride and found it impossible to move on the muddy lot. A large four-wheel drive farm tractor was hired locally to spot the show trucks. Even the tractor had its problems negotiating the mud, but the ride truck was finally moved toward its midway location.

The Kenworth truck with its huge ride trailer is now in place. The trailer frame is the ride frame so the foreman must now set down enough timber to support jacks and level the frame. Then the ride may be erected.

There is little doubt about the contents of the trailer on this military Reo M34. The midway and rail coaches must have needed lots of water. A small tank on the truck would have allowed it to tow wagons. These trucks had either a Reo or Continental six-cylinder gas engine, a five-speed transmission and two-range transfer case.

This circa 1950 Chevrolet model 6500 charged across a very soft lot with a full tank of water. The rear end sank to the axle. Four elephants could not move it. A dilemma faced circus management, either dump the water and lighten the truck, but make the mud worse, or, keep the water and try to move the full weight. Solution: they left the water in the tank and pulled from the rear, removing the truck along the same ruts it made when entering the field.

Heave Ho. This late 1970s GMC Astro diesel truck gets lots of help from two elephants on a very muddy lot. Circus trucks normally have the front bumper bolts replaced with eye bolts anticipating this sort of situation. Today, with good elephants in short supply, they are more likely to find a local tractor for hire.

The rear wheel of the big dark ride wagon at left had climbed the side of the flat car. Then the dual tires wedged down on the car frame. It was jammed in place. A circa 1965 Ford truck with a hydraulic crane was loaded behind the wagon to lift it off. This could not be done. Several tractors finally dragged the wagon to the end of the car where the wheel came loose.

This carnival usually moved on highway trucks, but for very long moves, used railroad-owned piggyback cars. A local drayman has been hired to unload the train. The drayman is driving a circa 1970 Ottawa Commando 30 yard spotter to haul the ride trailers. It has a Ford V-8 gas engine and an Allison automatic transmission.

The Ottawa Yard Spotter has a hydraulic lift under the fifth wheel and rigid rear suspension so it can back under a trailer, lift it off the fifth wheel support and drive away while the driver remains in the cab. Here it hauls a collapsed Giant Wheel off the train.

This trailer, mounting a Ferris Wheel, has little axle clearance and has hung on a fifth wheel support which did not drop flat on the car deck. The railroad has loaned a Pettibone hydraulic crane to lift the ride over the obstacle.

The crane supports the rear end of the Ferris Wheel trailer while the spotter truck carries the front end and unloading continues. Piggyback cars from the railroad system have only two fifth wheel supports, so can carry only two semi trailers regardless of trailer length. This is economical only for occasional use. Shows that own their own cars crowd many more wagons on a car, wasting very little space.

This truck appears to be an International 9670 hauling a type of folding big top seat unit. It has the seat sections stacked and unfolds by extending them to the right. The last one on top will reach the ground. These have become popular time and labor saving systems for medium sized shows.

Wild animal acts have a lot of equipment to transport—cages, an arena, pedestals and other props. They usually provide their own transportation. This trainer used a 1956 Ford with a stake trailer and sleeper cab.

This circa 1980 Chevrolet C60 is equipped with a single hammer stake driver and a single spool for the big top canvas. Some of the canvas remains on the spool while stakes are being driven. Edges of the spool have been cut straight. The truck pulls a trailer over the road and the straight edges allow sharp turns, avoiding the trailer bumping the spool.

White diesel number 77 carries the circus water tank and stake drivers and tows a trailer over the road. The stake drivers are powered by a small gas engine at the rear of the truck.

A mid-1950s Dodge K "Job Rated" truck handles the circus electric generating plant, or "hot wagon." Sides of the trailer fold neatly out to provide access to the electrical system. Most circuses such as Hagan Bros., found it expensive and inconvenient to tap into local utility power, so they carried their own generating equipment. Since carnivals remained for a week or more, some had only transformers in the hot wagon and connected to city power lines.

Trucks that transport the circus are parked beside the 3-ring big top. Number 40 is a Diamond T and carries lumber for the seat structure. To the right is a mid-1940s Chevrolet with what appears to be a personnel sleeper.

McGaws Motor Circus used only late model Ford trucks. In 1957 the circus had a promotional arrangement with Ford truck dealers who advertised on the midway. Some acts were also presented on Ford flat bed trucks as the trucks circled the arena. With this staging, patrons had each act directly in front of them during part of the routine.

Circus Vargas used a 1970 International Cargo Star 1710 to mount two hydraulic stake drivers. By mounting the drivers on the side of the truck overhanging the wheel, two stakes can be driven simultaneously with the guy rope spacing. The truck had International's V-8 gas engine of 478 cu. in. displacement.

Truck number 100, a mid-1940s Dodge, carries the big top poles, and probably some of the seat lumber as well. The spare center pole remains on a rack on top of the trailer. Dodge trucks of that period used six-cylinder flat-head gas engines derived from the passenger car designs.

The truck in the foreground is a 1950 GMC 300, as were most of the Biller Bros.' trucks. The workers in the background are pushing up the side poles of the big top. The emblem on the side of this GMC truck advertises that this circus (Biller Bros.) is the "Show that travels on GMC Trucks." General Motors had advertised on several occasions with various circuses and twice had a tent show of their own.

This circa-1970 White tandem axle truck is powered by a Cummins Diesel engine. It has threaded its way among the tent poles as workmen unloaded the reserve seats. The crane on the rear of the trailer was used to raise the seat sections and drop them on the ground. The unfortunate tent had suffered storm damage a few days before.

This early 1970s GMC truck has been customized by the circus, becoming a "Jack of all trades." In the body are carried an elephant and a dog act with some props. Behind the cab is an electric generator. Above the cab is a platform for all sorts of baggage. On the front of the platform is a jib crane used to load rolls of tent canvas. The crane is operated by an electric winch on the front bumper.

A GMC model 350 truck, circa 1950, arrives on the lot with a load of concession equipment. It appears that the trailer has been modified to include a sleeping compartment or "hot box" behind the cab.

This mid-1990s White truck carries two huge spools. The big top canvas is unlaced down the middle, then each half is folded lengthwise until it is the width of the spool. One folded strip is wound on each spool.

A crowd is attracted to this big Cummins-powered International truck, no doubt by the word "Hippopotamus" on the trailer. It is a Transtar F 4000, circa 1970. A variety of animals were carried and displayed in pens in front of the trailer.

The Clyde Beatty Cole Bros. Circus used a crane on the front of this 1971 Chevrolet C60 to load a roll of canvas from the side show tent. The weight of a tank of water on the truck stabilizes it when the load is lifted.

A human projectile act was featured on the Greater American Circus. This well-covered cannon was mounted on an early 1950s Federal truck. The truck had a support for the cannon barrel on the front bumper and two spotlights on the cab. The canvas cover on the cannon not only protected it from the weather but discouraged intrusion by the public. Cannons were mechanical catapults or sling shots with a powder charge for noise and smoke. The designs are often that of the performer and are closely guarded secrets.

A cannon truck waits by the back door of the big top. For the act, it will be driven straight in and the barrel elevated to a much higher angle. The truck has been so restyled to achieve an impressive appearance that identification is not possible from this photo. Such styling is fairly common since it adds a degree of mystery and suspense to the act.

An unusual cannon is styled to resemble a spacecraft, adding a modern, space age trend to the act. The truck appears to be a circa 1993 Iveco. The cannon is somewhat unusual in that it aims to the rear of the truck rather than over the cab.

This huge cannon truck is styled to resemble a fortress. The truck is a mid-1940s GMC Model AF with a GM six-cylinder gas engine providing 140 hp at 2400 rpm. Advertising boasted that the cannon would propel the performer over the Ferris wheel, a truly remarkable thrill act. At this location at least, it did not happen. Each day was declared to be too windy and the act was postponed.

This is a truck, but the space age styling of the "launch vehicle" is so extreme that identification is not possible. It is basically a cannon act but the barrel has been replaced by a "space capsule" in which the astronaut performer rides. The launch rail is elevated to a high angle for the act and the "astronaut" is ejected from the capsule when it reaches the end of the rail.

A mid-1980s Ford L 8000 truck transports the circus elephants in an oversize trailer, which appears to be a modified moving van. This type of trailer is preferred by circus owners who are concerned more by volume than by weight. Even the big elephants are transported in roomy comfort in the large van.

Two Chevrolet C60 trucks have illustrated trailers which form a banner line on the midway of the King Bros. Circus. Full color paintings on the tall trucks depict features of the side show. Use of trucks for a banner line required no labor other than parking the trucks.

A Cummins Diesel-powered mid-1980s International Transtar pulls this attractive midway food and drink vending trailer. Circus managers have learned that a bright, neat food service counter can boost sales as well as add to the colorful appearance of the show as patrons arrive.

Campa Bros. Circus had a nice fleet of cab forward Chevrolets in 1951 with various trailers. The big top in the background appears to accommodate two rings. To fit the show on a small lot, this or any circus might remove a section of canvas and one ring to reduce the size of the tent.

Coils of wire lie around Biller Bros. Circus hot wagon as show electricians prepare lights for the big top. The 1950 General Motors trucks have grill guards with the GMC monogram.

A mid-1980s White diesel carries Circus Vargas' midway food stand, four ticket booths and other baggage on the trailer. The tractor has a sleeper cab and cargo box. This is a good example of modern circus highway equipment.

In the background of this photo taken in 1951, one of the earliest spool trucks used by any circus unreels canvas. At left, side poles are unloaded from another truck, which is equipped with a stake driver. What appears to be a high platform is a cover, which is tipped over the driver when not in use.

An early 1940s Chevrolet arrives on a lot that appears to be a bit soft. These trucks had the 216 cu. in. Blue Flame six-cylinder gas engine. Trailer number 42 appears to be a personnel sleeper. In the 1950s, the Al G. Kelly and Miller Bros. Circus had one of the best-illustrated fleets of trucks of any circus. The trucks all had different designs. This photo was taken in 1951.

International T18 is designated as a fire safety unit because of the water tank and hose reel, but its main duty was towing wagons. It was a model 190 and had a Cummins HBS 600 diesel engine. With a belt-driven supercharger the engine produced 200 hp at 1800 rpm. The transmission had five speeds with a two-speed axle. These short, maneuverable trucks were preferred by drivers for towing long strings of wagons.

These International 190 trucks had to be the hardest working trucks in show business. The carnival moved the maximum number of wagons on each trip. If the route had no sharp turns or hills, they would often couple wagons, perhaps five or six, until the truck could not start the load. Then they would uncouple the last wagon and tell the driver to go ahead.

A 1959 International 190 soaks the dirt midway to settle dust. The spray bar is across the rear of the truck behind the wheels. The water tank is from an old Mack truck. During the week, while the midway was in operation, the truck supplied water to the grease joints, employees' trailers and the railroad coaches.

ADVERTISING CAR NO. 1

RINGLING BROS. AND BARNUM & BAILEY

An intense advertising campaign precedes each circus arrival. In years past the circus did much of its own promotion in the form of widely distributed posters in the downtown areas. Railroad shows had an advertising car, which transported the billing crew and supplies. It preceded the circus by two weeks and traveled hooked on the rear of passenger trains. This car was probably the last to be used for that purpose in 1956.

Truck-transported shows used a truck for the billing crew. This early 1950s GMC truck announces that it is the Advance Dept., a formal name for the billing crew, and was parked across the street from the railroad station. Advertising crews remained in town for the same number of days as the circus would perform there. Billposters did not drive around in the truck to post their ads, but walked, as they did from the railroad car.

This 1951 Ford F6 pulls a steam calliope decorated with solid wood carvings. It is inscribed, "Built In 1872" and was originally a horse-drawn wagon. The age is questionable but it is certainly old. The horse-drivers seat, footboard and brake wheel remain on top. It has been modified as a semi trailer and was driven over the highway.

The fireman stands on his little platform stoking the upright steam boiler as the calliope truck follows the elephants in the circus parade. This calliope had originally been a wagon with wooden wheels. The boiler was mounted over the rear axle. That was standard practice since the larger rear wheels and axle were better able to carry the weight. The elephants and the steam calliope were traditionally the last units in the parade order.

Steam rises from the calliope as the musician plays a tune that can be heard a mile away. The calliope concert announces the first performance of the circus. The truck is a mid-1950s Dodge with an attractively decorated semi trailer.

A 1959 International model 190 tank truck supplies water to the midway grease joint. This is its usual parking place when it is not doing other work. Notice the two bull rings on the front bumper in case it has to be towed, also the array of horns on the roof. These were officially for fire runs, but were mostly used to avoid stops when towing long strings of wagons.

This mid-1960s Chevrolet V-8 had an unusual trailer—a folded ski lift ride. It carried patrons over the midway in suspended chairs. Loaded in front of it is a Pettibone four-wheel drive hydraulic crane. The crane is loaded on the front of the flat car with the boom extending over the car coupling to save space.

A late 1950s International truck with a hydraulic crane behind the cab prepares to lift part of a midway ride into position. This truck has International's big V-8 gas engine and hauled a ride semi trailer on the train.

An emblem on this mid-1950s Ford says "Big Job" and it certainly did that for the carnival. Its closed body must have carried valuable supplies since it is parked in a fenced area with one of the office wagons. The wagon has a window with bars such as bank tellers use, indicating cash is handled there. The truck has Ford's V-8 gas engine based on the Lincoln block and was normally used to pull strings of wagons.

This broad view of King Bros. Circus lot includes many interesting vehicles. At left is a 1942 Buick sedan. Next is a 1937 Chevrolet truck, which is the hot wagon. Truck number 60 is the pole truck, a late 1940s Federal, with the spare center pole on top. At right, beyond the elephants, is a late 1940s Spartan Manor trailer. Spartans were all-aluminum and were one of the premium trailers of the time.

Carson Barnes Circus used a pre-WWII armored car as a stake driver. Its four-wheel drive feature allowed it to move on muddy lots without help. Officially designated as the M3A1 Scout Car, it was built by White. Most were equipped with the Hercules JXD six-cylinder gas engine producing 113 hp at 3000 rpm. A few had the Buda 6 DT 317 diesel engine producing 90 hp at 2300 rpm. The M3A1 preceded the half-track as a standard armored vehicle. The rear armor has been removed to allow the stake bin and driver to be mounted. The roller on the bumper was standard military equipment, permitting the vehicle to climb obstacles.

Any circus tries to be as independent as possible and not rely on local services, but occasionally local trucks have to be hired to move wagons from the train to the circus lot. This hired tow truck is a former army 2 1/2-ton 6X6 model AFKK built by General Motors. It is a pre-WWII design with a civilian cab and hood. The later CCKW wartime model had military sheet metal. The owner has installed a long body so workmen have to crawl under it to couple the cage wagon.

A circus occasionally finds a situation where local police will not allow Caterpillars with steel tracks on the pavement and the haul to the lot, in this case four miles, makes it inconvenient to shuttle the shows own flat wagons back to the train. A local hauling company has been hired to move the Cats. They supplied a very large flat wagon that looks as though it could carry two tractors. It is pulled by a mid-1940s FWD T32 truck powered by a Waukesha MKR 96-hp six-cylinder gas engine. It had a five-speed transmission.

The Johnny J. Jones carnival used a WWII army surplus truck to tow wagons and supply water on the lot. The water tank was added by the carnival. This was General Motors model DOK low silhouette 4X4. It had GM's 360 cu. in. gas engine providing 160 hp at 3400 rpm. The original rag top cab has been replaced with a metal roof. It appears to have the original Gar Wood winch mounted behind the bumper. The wagon D3 is one of the hot wagons, which light the midway. In view is the Caterpillar 75 KW electric set. The Chevrolet on the right is a locally hired dump truck towing wagon number 81 to the crossing.

A GM DOK former army truck is being used to haul wagons up the runs onto the train by means of a cable hooked to the wagon. The truck was shifted to low gear, low range, four-wheel drive for this job. With a full water tank it still slipped on the gravel roadbed when heavier wagons were loaded.

A former army General Motors DOK truck is about to pull a carnival wagon up the runs. The DOK had a five-speed transmission with a two-speed transfer case. The wagon will be steered by hand on the train. On the right a locally hired GM truck has brought another wagon from the lot. This carnival normally hired several local trucks if the rail crossing was any distance from the show grounds.

One of the big top center poles is hoisted by this former military 2 1/2-ton 6X6 truck. It is a WWII General Motors CCKW. This one has a metal roof and full doors on the cab, whereas most WWII production were rag tops. These trucks were the workhorses of that war. It had GM's six-cylinder 270 cu. in. gas engine, rated at 120 hp at 3600 rpm for civilian trucks. The army version was governed at 2750 rpm allowing 45 mph top speed in 5th gear (overdrive). Front-end winches were standard, supplied either by Heil or Gar Wood. The crane was added by the circus.

Rogers Bros. Circus used this military surplus half-track as its mechanics truck, as evidenced by the load of tires and parts. It was the last vehicle to leave the lot each morning. If a truck had a flat or broke down, the crew of the half-track would either repair it or tow it to the next town. It also served as a tractor to move trucks on muddy lots. When its rubber belt tracks wore down it was carried on a truck and unloaded only for muddy lots.

Whale exhibits were popular in the 1930s. One or two railroad cars would carry an embalmed, or perhaps a fake whale, and other curiosities. They were parked in railroad stations. In the post-war years a few truck-transported whale shows displayed smaller whales in parking lots. This circa 1970 Kenworth carried a 37-ft long, 16-ton sperm whale. The whale, injected with embalming fluid, remained in the trailer. Customers ascended the outboard platform to view the big creature.

Commercial truckers are being used more frequently to haul carnival trailers and find themselves with some unusual loads behind them. This mid-1990s Freightliner is ready to leave with two large, brightly painted rides, which will get lots of attention on the highway. Carnivals move only once a week or less often and some are finding it more economical to hire professional truckers than to own and maintain their own trucks.

A 1985 Chevrolet W7 Tiltmaster truck climbs the runs with a string of wagons behind it. It had a Caterpillar model 3208 V-8 diesel engine. The body carries mechanics supplies. Behind the body is a spare railroad wheel and axle assembly that provides plenty of adhesive weight when the truck is towing wagons.

A bullnose International tows a string of carnival wagons off the train. When not towing wagons it is a sanitation truck, with pumps and a tank for cleaning out waste tanks of midway restrooms and the show's railroad coaches. It is a mid-1950s International RC 160.

A circus bus is not a vehicle of choice for towing wagons, but this Bluebird Coach is heading up the runs with two wagons, getting a lot of help from a tractor in the rear. The bus is one of several vehicles loaded at intervals on the cut of flat cars to provide lead vehicles to steer strings of wagons. This avoids steering them by hand. The bus transports circus personnel from the train to the arena where the performance is given. Rail yards are often far from the downtown building and city bus service is either inconvenient or unavailable. It is called the Gilly Bus, which means local transportation on the circus. The custom of providing bus service goes back to the very early days of the circus.

A 1990 Isuzu truck heads for the train with three wagons. The first wagon carries rolled rubber mats used to carpet the performance area, providing safe footing. This is one of the heavier wagons as indicated by the triple tires. Most of the wagons are of low profile design in order to enter doors of buildings. The truck has a fiberglass tank, which prevents rust in the water. It is an Isuzu FTR with an Isuzu six-cylinder turbocharged diesel engine, 170 hp at 3000 rpm. The transmission is a five-speed manual.

This circa 1990 Kenworth carries a big double spool body. The spool body was stamped "Wayne Sanguin 1951," making it one of the earliest of this type, and a very durable one. Sanguin was one of the early designers of the canvas reel. Here the canvas has been unloaded and the heavy truck is being used as a "dead man" to anchor the main cable that runs the length of the big top. The truck is lettered "To The Circus" and has a large arrow painted on the side. If the lot were far from the main highway, this truck would be used as a billboard, parked at the highway with the arrow pointing to the circus entrance.

A 1951 Ford spool truck peels out its load of canvas as it passes the center poles. Spool trucks move forward to unload, backward to load. This one had been battered around the hood and fenders, no doubt from gear being thrown off the rack above the cab.

Days of glory lead but to the junkyard. This veteran Mack AC rests with a row of obsolete wagons in the Sarasota quarters, no longer getting the attention it received when it helped move the big circus. The radiator assembly and front frame cross member have been used to keep other trucks running. The aluminum crankcase of the gas engine can be seen below the hood. This was the first of the bulldogs retired because it had one of the smallest water tanks, and a wooden tank at that. The old truck saw service from the late 1920s until 1942.

Truck number 243, a 1931 International A5, carried the power dishwasher for the circus cookhouse. It last saw service in 1945 or 1946. It had an International six-cylinder gas engine rated at 67 hp. Initially the truck engine powered the dishwasher system. When WWII began a diesel engine was mounted in the truck as washer power. Note that the exhaust has been routed under the body, then forward and up over the cab.

Mack AC4 number 239 saw its last season of service in 1946. It had the shortest wheelbase offered by Mack—120 inches. Since it had not been converted to diesel power it was the first of the old Macks to be replaced after WWII. The water tank replaced a wooden tank on another truck. Its neighbors are cage wagons last used for the "Hold Your Horses" feature of the 1943 circus performance.

MORE TITLES FROM ICONOGRAFIX:

AMERICAN CULTURE

- AMERICAN SERVICE STATIONS 1935-1943 PHOTO ARCHIVE — ISBN 1-882256-27-1
- COCA-COLA: A HISTORY IN PHOTOGRAPHS 1930-1969 — ISBN 1-882256-46-8
- COCA-COLA: ITS VEHICLES IN PHOTOGRAPHS 1930-1969 — ISBN 1-882256-47-6
- PHILLIPS 66 1945-1954 PHOTO ARCHIVE — ISBN 1-882256-42-5

AUTOMOTIVE

- CADILLAC 1948-1964 PHOTO ALBUM — ISBN 1-882256-83-2
- CAMARO 1967-2000 PHOTO ARCHIVE — ISBN 1-58388-032-1
- CLASSIC AMERICAN LIMOUSINES 1955-2000 PHOTO ARCHIVE — ISBN 1-58388-041-0
- CORVAIR by CHEVROLET EXP. & PROD. CARS 1957-1969 LUDVIGSEN LIBRARY SERIES — ISBN 1-58388-058-5
- CORVETTE THE EXOTIC EXPERIMENTAL CARS, LUDVIGSEN LIBRARY SERIES — ISBN 1-58388-017-8
- CORVETTE PROTOTYPES & SHOW CARS PHOTO ALBUM — ISBN 1-882256-77-8
- EARLY FORD V-8S 1932-1942 PHOTO ALBUM — ISBN 1-882256-97-2
- IMPERIAL 1955-1963 PHOTO ARCHIVE — ISBN 1-882256-22-0
- IMPERIAL 1964-1968 PHOTO ARCHIVE — ISBN 1-882256-23-9
- LINCOLN MOTOR CARS 1920-1942 PHOTO ARCHIVE — ISBN 1-882256-57-3
- LINCOLN MOTOR CARS 1946-1960 PHOTO ARCHIVE — ISBN 1-882256-58-1
- PACKARD MOTOR CARS 1935-1942 PHOTO ARCHIVE — ISBN 1-882256-44-1
- PACKARD MOTOR CARS 1946-1958 PHOTO ARCHIVE — ISBN 1-882256-45-X
- PONTIAC DREAM CARS, SHOW CARS & PROTOTYPES 1928-1998 PHOTO ALBUM — ISBN 1-882256-93-X
- PONTIAC FIREBIRD TRANS-AM 1969-1999 PHOTO ALBUM — ISBN 1-882256-95-6
- PONTIAC FIREBIRD 1967-2000 PHOTO HISTORY — ISBN 1-58388-028-3
- STUDEBAKER 1933-1942 PHOTO ARCHIVE — ISBN 1-882256-24-7
- ULTIMATE CORVETTE TRIVIA CHALLENGE — ISBN 1-58388-035-6

BUSES

- BUSES OF MOTOR COACH INDUSTRIES 1932-2000 PHOTO ARCHIVE — ISBN 1-58388-039-9
- FLXIBLE TRANSIT BUSES 1953-1995 PHOTO ARCHIVE — ISBN 1-58388-053-4
- THE GENERAL MOTORS NEW LOOK BUS PHOTO ARCHIVE — ISBN 1-58388-007-0
- GREYHOUND BUSES 1914-2000 PHOTO ARCHIVE — ISBN 1-58388-027-5
- MACK® BUSES 1900-1960 PHOTO ARCHIVE* — ISBN 1-58388-020-8
- TRAILWAYS BUSES 1936-2001 PHOTO ARCHIVE — ISBN 1-58388-029-1
- TROLLEY BUSES 1910-2001 PHOTO ARCHIVE — ISBN 1-58388-057-7
- YELLOW COACH BUSES 1923-1943 PHOTO ARCHIVE — ISBN 1-58388-054-2

EMERGENCY VEHICLES

- AMERICAN LAFRANCE 700 SERIES 1945-1952 PHOTO ARCHIVE — ISBN 1-882256-90-5
- AMERICAN LAFRANCE 700 SERIES 1945-1952 PHOTO ARCHIVE VOLUME 2 — ISBN 1-58388-025-9
- AMERICAN LAFRANCE 700 & 800 SERIES 1953-1958 PHOTO ARCHIVE — ISBN 1-882256-91-3
- AMERICAN LAFRANCE 900 SERIES 1958-1964 PHOTO ARCHIVE — ISBN 1-58388-002-X
- CROWN FIRECOACH 1951-1985 PHOTO ARCHIVE — ISBN 1-58388-047-X
- CLASSIC AMERICAN AMBULANCES 1900-1979 PHOTO ARCHIVE — ISBN 1-882256-94-8
- CLASSIC AMERICAN FUNERAL VEHICLES 1900-1980 PHOTO ARCHIVE — ISBN 1-58388-016-X
- CLASSIC SEAGRAVE 1935-1951 PHOTO ARCHIVE — ISBN 1-58388-034-8
- FIRE CHIEF CARS 1900-1997 PHOTO ALBUM — ISBN 1-882256-87-5
- HEAVY RESCUE TRUCKS 1931-2000 PHOTO GALLERY — ISBN 1-58388-045-3
- INDUSTRIAL AND PRIVATE FIRE APPARATUS 1925-2001 PHOTO ARCHIVE — ISBN 1-58388-049-6
- LOS ANGELES CITY FIRE APPARATUS 1953 - 1999 PHOTO ARCHIVE — ISBN 1-58388-012-7
- MACK MODEL C FIRE TRUCKS 1957-1967 PHOTO ARCHIVE* — ISBN 1-58388-014-3
- MACK MODEL CF FIRE TRUCKS 1967-1981 PHOTO ARCHIVE* — ISBN 1-882256-63-8
- MACK MODEL L FIRE TRUCKS 1940-1954 PHOTO ARCHIVE* — ISBN 1-882256-86-7
- MAXIM FIRE APPARATUS 1914-1989 PHOTO ARCHIVE — ISBN 1-58388-050-X
- NAVY & MARINE CORPS FIRE APPARATUS 1836 -2000 PHOTO GALLERY — ISBN 1-58388-031-3
- PIERCE ARROW FIRE APPARATUS 1979-1998 PHOTO ARCHIVE — ISBN 1-58388-023-2
- POLICE CARS: RESTORING, COLLECTING & SHOWING AMERICA'S FINEST SEDANS — ISBN 1-58388-046-1
- SEAGRAVE 70TH ANNIVERSARY SERIES PHOTO ARCHIVE — ISBN 1-58388-001-1
- VOLUNTEER & RURAL FIRE APPARATUS PHOTO GALLERY — ISBN 1-58388-005-4
- WARD LAFRANCE FIRE TRUCKS 1918-1978 PHOTO ARCHIVE — ISBN 1-58388-013-5
- WILDLAND FIRE APPARATUS 1940-2001 PHOTO GALLERY — ISBN 1-58388-056-9
- YOUNG FIRE EQUIPMENT 1932-1991 PHOTO ARCHIVE — ISBN 1-58388-015-1

RACING

- GT40 PHOTO ARCHIVE — ISBN 1-882256-64-6
- INDY CARS OF THE 1950s, LUDVIGSEN LIBRARY SERIES — ISBN 1-58388-018-6
- INDY CARS OF THE 1960s, LUDVIGSEN LIBRARY SERIES — ISBN 1-58388-052-6
- INDIANAPOLIS RACING CARS OF FRANK KURTIS 1941-1963 PHOTO ARCHIVE — ISBN 1-58388-026-7
- JUAN MANUEL FANGIO WORLD CHAMPION DRIVER SERIES PHOTO ALBUM — ISBN 1-58388-008-9
- LE MANS 1950 PHOTO ARCHIVE THE BRIGGS CUNNINGHAM CAMPAIGN — ISBN 1-882256-21-2
- MARIO ANDRETTI WORLD CHAMPION DRIVER SERIES PHOTO ALBUM — ISBN 1-58388-009-7
- NOVI V-8 INDY CARS 1941-1965 LUDVIGSEN LIBRARY SERIES — ISBN 1-58388-037-2
- SEBRING 12-HOUR RACE 1970 PHOTO ARCHIVE — ISBN 1-882256-20-4
- VANDERBILT CUP RACE 1936 & 1937 PHOTO ARCHIVE — ISBN 1-882256-66-2

RAILWAYS

- CHICAGO, ST. PAUL, MINNEAPOLIS & OMAHA RAILWAY 1880-1940 PHOTO ARCHIVE — ISBN 1-882256-67-0
- CHICAGO & NORTH WESTERN RAILWAY 1975-1995 PHOTO ARCHIVE — ISBN 1-882256-76-X
- GREAT NORTHERN RAILWAY 1945-1970 PHOTO ARCHIVE — ISBN 1-882256-56-5
- GREAT NORTHERN RAILWAY 1945-1970 VOL 2 PHOTO ARCHIVE — ISBN 1-882256-79-4
- MILWAUKEE ROAD 1850-1960 PHOTO ARCHIVE — ISBN 1-882256-61-1
- MILWAUKEE ROAD DEPOTS 1856-1954 PHOTO ARCHIVE — ISBN 1-58388-040-2
- SHOW TRAINS OF THE 20TH CENTURY — ISBN 1-58388-030-5
- SOO LINE 1975-1992 PHOTO ARCHIVE — ISBN 1-882256-68-9
- TRAINS OF THE TWIN PORTS, DULUTH-SUPERIOR IN THE 1950s PHOTO ARCHIVE — ISBN 1-58388-003-8
- TRAINS OF THE CIRCUS 1872-1956 — ISBN 1-58388-024-0
- TRAINS of the UPPER MIDWEST PHOTO ARCHIVE STEAM&DIESEL in the1950S&1960S — ISBN 1-58388-036-4
- WISCONSIN CENTRAL LIMITED 1987-1996 PHOTO ARCHIVE — ISBN 1-882256-75-1
- WISCONSIN CENTRAL RAILWAY 1871-1909 PHOTO ARCHIVE — ISBN 1-882256-78-6

TRUCKS

- BEVERAGE TRUCKS 1910-1975 PHOTO ARCHIVE — ISBN 1-882256-60-3
- BROCKWAY TRUCKS 1948-1961 PHOTO ARCHIVE* — ISBN 1-882256-55-7
- CHEVROLET EL CAMINO PHOTO HISTORY INCL GMC SPRINT & CABALLERO — ISBN 1-58388-044-5
- CIRCUS AND CARNIVAL TRUCKS 1923-2000 PHOTO ARCHIVE — ISBN 1-58388-048-8
- DODGE PICKUPS 1939-1978 PHOTO ALBUM — ISBN 1-882256-82-4
- DODGE POWER WAGONS 1940-1980 PHOTO ARCHIVE — ISBN 1-882256-89-1
- DODGE POWER WAGON PHOTO HISTORY — ISBN 1-58388-019-4
- DODGE RAM TRUCKS 1994-2001 PHOTO HISTORY — ISBN 1-58388-051-8
- DODGE TRUCKS 1929-1947 PHOTO ARCHIVE — ISBN 1-882256-36-0
- DODGE TRUCKS 1948-1960 PHOTO ARCHIVE — ISBN 1-882256-37-9
- FORD HEAVY DUTY TRUCKS 1948-1998 PHOTO HISTORY — ISBN 1-58388-043-7
- JEEP 1941-2000 PHOTO ARCHIVE — ISBN 1-58388-021-6
- JEEP PROTOTYPES & CONCEPT VEHICLES PHOTO ARCHIVE — ISBN 1-58388-033-X
- LOGGING TRUCKS 1915-1970 PHOTO ARCHIVE — ISBN 1-882256-59-X
- MACK MODEL AB PHOTO ARCHIVE* — ISBN 1-882256-18-2
- MACK AP SUPER-DUTY TRUCKS 1926-1938 PHOTO ARCHIVE* — ISBN 1-882256-54-9
- MACK MODEL B 1953-1966 VOL 1 PHOTO ARCHIVE* — ISBN 1-882256-19-0
- MACK MODEL B 1953-1966 VOL 2 PHOTO ARCHIVE* — ISBN 1-882256-34-4
- MACK EB-EC-ED-EE-EF-EG-DE 1936-1951 PHOTO ARCHIVE* — ISBN 1-882256-29-8
- MACK EH-EJ-EM-EQ-ER-ES 1936-1950 PHOTO ARCHIVE* — ISBN 1-882256-39-5
- MACK FC-FCSW-NW 1936-1947 PHOTO ARCHIVE* — ISBN 1-882256-28-X
- MACK FG-FH-FJ-FK-FN-FP-FT-FW 1937-1950 PHOTO ARCHIVE* — ISBN 1-882256-35-2
- MACK LF-LH-LJ-LM-LT 1940-1956 PHOTO ARCHIVE* — ISBN 1-882256-38-7
- MACK TRUCKS PHOTO GALLERY* — ISBN 1-882256-88-3
- NEW CAR CARRIERS 1910-1998 PHOTO ALBUM — ISBN 1-882256-98-0
- PLYMOUTH COMMERCIAL VEHICLES PHOTO ARCHIVE — ISBN 1-58388-004-6
- REFUSE TRUCKS PHOTO ARCHIVE — ISBN 1-58388-042-9
- STUDEBAKER /5TRUCKS 1927-1940 PHOTO ARCHIVE — ISBN 1-882256-40-9
- STUDEBAKER TRUCKS 1941-1964 PHOTO ARCHIVE — ISBN 1-882256-41-7
- WHITE TRUCKS 1900-1937 PHOTO ARCHIVE — ISBN 1-882256-80-8

TRACTORS & CONSTRUCTION EQUIPMENT

- CASE TRACTORS 1912-1959 PHOTO ARCHIVE — ISBN 1-882256-32-8
- CATERPILLAR PHOTO GALLERY — ISBN 1-882256-70-0
- CATERPILLAR POCKET GUIDE THE TRACK-TYPE TRACTORS 1925-1957 — ISBN 1-58388-022-4
- CATERPILLAR D-2 & R-2 PHOTO ARCHIVE — ISBN 1-882256-99-9
- CATERPILLAR D-8 1933-1974 PHOTO ARCHIVE INCLUDING DIESEL 75 & RD-8 — ISBN 1-882256-96-4
- CATERPILLAR MILITARY TRACTORS VOLUME 1 PHOTO ARCHIVE — ISBN 1-882256-16-6
- CATERPILLAR MILITARY TRACTORS VOLUME 2 PHOTO ARCHIVE — ISBN 1-882256-17-4
- CATERPILLAR SIXTY PHOTO ARCHIVE — ISBN 1-882256-05-0
- CATERPILLAR TEN PHOTO ARCHIVE INCLUDING 7C FIFTEEN & HIGH FIFTEEN — ISBN 1-58388-011-9
- CATERPILLAR THIRTY PHOTO ARCHIVE 2ND ED. INC. BEST THIRTY, 6G THIRTY & R-4 — ISBN 1-58388-006-2
- CLETRAC AND OLIVER CRAWLERS PHOTO ARCHIVE — ISBN 1-882256-43-3
- CLASSIC AMERICAN STEAMROLLERS 1871-1935 PHOTO ARCHIVE — ISBN 1-58388-038-0
- FARMALL CUB PHOTO ARCHIVE — ISBN 1-882256-71-9
- FARMALL F- SERIES PHOTO ARCHIVE — ISBN 1-882256-02-6
- FARMALL MODEL H PHOTO ARCHIVE — ISBN 1-882256-03-4
- FARMALL MODEL M PHOTO ARCHIVE — ISBN 1-882256-15-8
- FARMALL REGULAR PHOTO ARCHIVE — ISBN 1-882256-14-X
- FARMALL SUPER SERIES PHOTO ARCHIVE — ISBN 1-882256-49-2
- FORDSON 1917-1928 PHOTO ARCHIVE — ISBN 1-882256-33-6
- HART-PARR PHOTO ARCHIVE — ISBN 1-882256-08-5
- HOLT TRACTORS PHOTO ARCHIVE — ISBN 1-882256-10-7
- INTERNATIONAL TRACTRACTOR PHOTO ARCHIVE — ISBN 1-882256-48-4
- INTERNATIONAL TD CRAWLERS 1933-1962 PHOTO ARCHIVE — ISBN 1-882256-72-7
- JOHN DEERE MODEL A PHOTO ARCHIVE — ISBN 1-882256-12-3
- JOHN DEERE MODEL B PHOTO ARCHIVE — ISBN 1-882256-01-8
- JOHN DEERE MODEL D PHOTO ARCHIVE — ISBN 1-882256-00-X
- JOHN DEERE 30 SERIES PHOTO ARCHIVE — ISBN 1-882256-13-1
- MINNEAPOLIS-MOLINE U-SERIES PHOTO ARCHIVE — ISBN 1-882256-07-7
- OLIVER TRACTORS PHOTO ARCHIVE — ISBN 1-882256-09-3
- RUSSELL GRADERS PHOTO ARCHIVE — ISBN 1-882256-11-5
- TWIN CITY TRACTOR PHOTO ARCHIVE — ISBN 1-882256-06-9

All Iconografix books are available from direct mail specialty book dealers and bookstores worldwide, or can be ordered from the publisher. For book trade and distribution information or to add your name to our mailing list and receive a **FREE CATALOG** contact:

Iconografix, PO Box 446, Hudson, Wisconsin, 54016   Telephone: (715) 381-9755, (800) 289-3504 (USA), Fax: (715) 381-9756

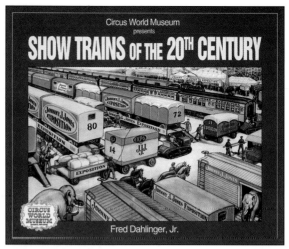
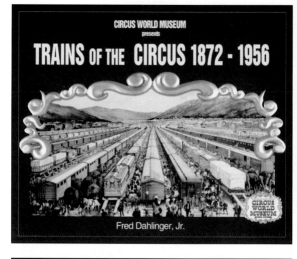
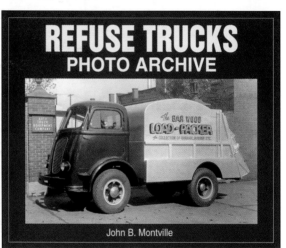
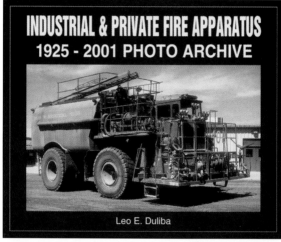

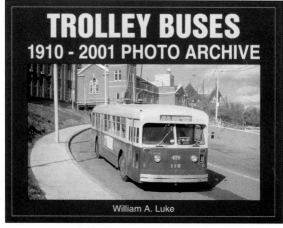